Be Hopeful!

Published by Honeysuckle Hill Publishing.
The United States of America.
Printed in the United States of America.

Scripture quotations are from the *New Revised Standard Version Bible: Catholic Edition*, (NRSV) copyright © 1989, 1993 by the National Council of the Churches of Christ in the United States of America. Used by permission. All rights reserved. Credits acknowledged with other quotations.

Genre: *Spirituality, Psychology, Quality of Life*

Library of Congress Cataloging-in-Publication Data
Name Gilner, Marguerite Patricia, Author. 1942-
Title: *Be Hopeful: An Alphabetical Anthology*

Cover design, layout design, and photographic art: Marguerite Patricia Gilner

ISBN: 978-1-63760-743-5 (Hardcover)
ISBN: 979-8-74321-241-5 (Paperback)
Library of Congress Control Number: 20209250

Author's email address: Seasideretreat@comcast.net

Be Hopeful

An Alphabetical Anthology

By

Marguerite Patricia Gilner

Dedication

In loving memory of my dear sister, Ann.
You will always have a special place in my heart.

Table of Contents

Preface

THE RESILIENCE OF THE HUMAN SPIRIT

The history of our ancestors reminds us of the resilience of the human spirit. Recorded stories share accounts of courage and survival during the most devastating times. *Be Hopeful* is an outgrowth of a conviction that our spiritual beliefs, affirmations, and positive thinking can help sustain us during difficult times. The COVID-19, causing a pandemic, took us by surprise. For over a year, the pandemic changed the way we lived, worked, and socialized. It changed our way of being. The virus introduced us to an element of fear, unlike anything we ever experienced. As we *slowed down* and *stayed home*, we had time to reflect on the meaning and purpose of our lives' journeys. Now, over a year later, we look back with a feeling of relief and a sense of hope. The COVID-19 vaccine offers promise for us to return to some feeling of normalcy. As we review the year's happenings, we see that a favorable outcome came in the inner strength we gained. It gave us the courage to seek a better *quality of life*, even during unusual circumstances. Fear and mystery created a panic as offices, churches, and social venues shut down to control the disease's spread. Yet, the anxiety produced by fear and the many unknowns caused us to rely on our inner strength and live in the present, appreciating the *gift of today*.

This book's reflections provide insight and meditation opportunities on some of the essential principles we value and practice. While writing, I recognized a pattern was unfolding with themes that covered most of the alphabet. I took that concept and created an alphabetical anthology of reflections to challenge and motivate us to seek answers to the questions we ponder. Writing *Be Hopeful* has challenged me to reflect on life-changing values. I hope the reflections will give you solace and peace.

As we imagine a future filled with hope, the images of struggles and hardships caused by the coronavirus are fresh on our minds. We don't want to return to a pre-pandemic state but hope to go forward and appreciate living a more intentional lifestyle.

One of the positive outcomes of the pandemic was having the *gift of time* to slow down emotionally and take notice of our hectic lives. The quarantine became a time of discernment, as we sought after a spiritual quest. This quest brought us to a fork in the road; aware that our decisions determine the direction and lifestyle we choose. How we live, what we believe, and how we relate to those who accompany us determine the choices we make. In the process, our inner resilience unveils strengths unimagined until tested. Saying *"yes"* to one path is saying *"no"* to other paths. Harvey Cox tells us, *"Not to decide is to decide."* We are always making decisions, even when we make the decision not to decide.

Some discovered new gifts and talents during the *stay home* phase, some found *new hope*, and some experienced *greater peace* by opting for a simpler, less complicated lifestyle. Sadly, many experienced heartaches and losses that were unexpected. Some, more than others, suffered enormous losses, including the death of loved ones and friends. COVID-19 will go down in history as a time that brought us to our knees. Nevertheless, our resilient spirit sought a peaceful calm while living with the uncertainty of this tragedy.

As I pen this *Preface* on Easter Sunday, my heart rejoices with hopefulness. Finally, there is hope on the horizon. Spring is upon us. Tiny buds are appearing on the barren branches. The delicate croci and sun-kissed daffodils are springing up through the recently thawed earth. These images announce a time of rebirth, a new beginning. Our hopefulness emerges as we pay attention to our inner emotions, tested and embraced during the quiet time of our *stay home* phase. In unexpected ways, the pandemic has been a blessing in disguise, allowing us time to slow down and discover the *monk* hidden deep in the recesses of our being. From this day forward, may your life be a story of resilience, optimism, and joy!

Happy Easter! Wishing you blessings filled with renewed hope and peace.

Take gentle care,

Marguerite Patricia Gilner

Easter Sunday, April 4, 2021
Milton, Delaware

And the People Stayed Home

Kitty O'Meara

(Printed with permission.)

And the people stayed home.

And read books and listened, and rested and exercised.

And made art and played games.

And learned new ways of being and were still.

And listened more deeply.

Some meditated, some prayed, some danced.

Some met their shadows.

And the people began to think differently.

And the people healed.

And in the absence of people living in ignorant,

Dangerous, mindless and heartless ways,

The earth began to heal.

And when the danger passed,

And the people joined together again,

They grieved their losses, and made new choices,

And dreamed new images,

And created new ways to live and heal the earth fully,

As they had been healed.

Prologue

"HOPE IS THE HEARTBEAT OF THE SOUL."

Michelle Horst

With hope in our hearts, we can weather the emotionally and mentally challenging storms that come our way and live to see a beautiful sunrise welcoming a new day. The word *"hope"* has been my mantra since I was a young adult. It is a powerful word because of all it implies. I have used the word *hope* as part of my passwords, access codes on bank accounts, locks, and computers. I am not sure when *hope* became so meaningful to me, but it dates back to my early twenties. *Hope* has been a powerful force in helping me survive significant challenges. Blessed with a positive and hopeful attitude, I have survived unusual crises on several occasions. No matter how bleak a situation, I believed that in the end, I would bounce back. Remarkably, bouncing back has been a welcomed occurrence throughout my life.

My personal analogy of *hope* is that of a *breeze*. You can feel a breeze but not see it. A breeze is invisible to the eye but gentle to our somatosensory perception that refreshes our being. So, also with the concept of hope. *Hope* has the quality that boosts our spirits and gives us the courage to work through a process to survive the difficult times. Without hope, we are void of the courage to fight the good fight.

I was diagnosed with advanced-stage ovarian cancer in my thirties. The diagnosis came on the heels of a three-month hospitalization with endocarditis. My poor prognosis devastated me. The chemotherapy treatments were for palliative care to buy me some time, not to cure. After being discharged from the hospital from my first surgery, I wanted something tangible, a visible reminder to be hopeful, trust in God, and believe in miracles. I went to a jewelry store in downtown Baltimore a few blocks from where I lived, searching for an anchor to wear as a necklace. I found one that seemed perfect, but it was too expensive. I kept revisiting the jewelry store and checking to see if it was still there. The store owner was an elderly gentleman who observed my frequent visits and finally asked me why I was interested in the anchor necklace. I told him about my diagnosis and how I wanted to wear an anchor I could cling to as my sign of hope. He offered me a deal: He would reduce the price if I prayed for him (he

"IN THE END,
IT'S NOT
THE YEARS IN
YOUR LIFE
THAT COUNTS.
IT'S THE LIFE
IN YOUR YEARS."

Abraham Lincoln

was also battling cancer). We had an agreement, and I left the store wearing the anchor necklace. I only took it off when I was in surgery. It was a tangible sign that accompanied me through my many hospitalizations, chemotherapy treatments, and subsequent surgery visits. Almost forty years later, I still wear the anchor necklace as a visible sign of hope and a reminder of my remarkable healing.

As I worked on this book's design, I incorporated the anchor's image with daffodils and fresh falling snow to symbolize the mystery and power of hopefulness. The anchor, a Christian symbol of *hope*, represents the stability that keeps us from drifting aimlessly. The daffodil survives the late winter snowfall to blossom into a vibrant spring flower. And snow has a magical quality, falling softly and gracefully, blanketing the landscape with a glistening glow. I have incorporated these images to create a design that, for me, epitomizes renewed hope.

The coronavirus has impacted our lives and changed our concept of normalcy. It came without notice, and then suddenly, COVID-19 challenged us to live life differently. Many thought it was only for a few weeks or a month, but it has been more than a year of social distancing, wearing masks, and staying home. And, we have discovered things about ourselves we never imagined.

The isolation gave us an invitation to look inward and to question our priorities and values. The vaccine is our hope. This hope is real, but we still have a long way to go. The vaccine controls the spread and severity of the virus, making it possible to hug once again, embrace those we love, enjoy friendships, and celebrate special times. We have learned to seek balance through it all and to be patient as we await some resemblance of normalcy. With hope in our hearts, we feel confident and dare to believe in a brighter future.

Be Hopeful has twenty-six short reflections, one for each letter of the alphabet. Each reflection addresses a meaningful theme to enhance your *quality of life*. The reflections contain pearls of wisdom to touch your heart and empower you to live your most amazing life throughout all its seasons. The journaling pages are for you to jot down your feelings in response to the reflections. The journaling section is called *"Just for Today"* to remind you to be attentive to the activities of your day. I hope you can embrace the moment, focus on being aware of all that is happening now, mindful of the moments clustered together to shape the atmosphere and temperament of your day.

Our lives have changed due to the challenges we have lived through for more than a year. Life will never be quite the same, only more profound because of the shared experiences that bonded us together, helping us find light in the shades of darkness. We have fine-tuned our empathic nature to see others differently and to love more tenderly.

In our noisy world, it behooves us to cultivate quiet. For me, a quiet walk on the beach renews my spirit. I remind myself to breathe, slow down, put aside worries, and listen to the sounds of silence echoing with the rhyme of the splashing waves. Beaches are peaceful places, void of the noise of the hustle and bustle of our chaotic world. Stamping footprints in the sand and watching the ocean surf erase them helps me appreciate the sacredness of the present moment. Like the disappearing footprints on the beach, our lives are but a fleeting imprint on this world. Breathe slowly. Take a Deep Breath...Breathe.

IN THE MIDST OF WINTER,
I HAVE DISCOVERED
WITHIN ME
AN INVINCIBLE SPRING
FILLED WITH RENEWED HOPE.

Aging with Grace

Aging with Grace: The Gift and the Struggle

We may fear getting older, but many blessings grace us as we slow down and enjoy the evening years of our lives. Aging is an extraordinary process that allows us to become a better version of our authentic selves. It doesn't have to be a barrier to a fulfilling and happy life. We cannot control some things in life, and aging's physical diminishment is among them. If we have the good fortune to grow old, we get to celebrate the journey into our tranquil and noble years. Not everyone has that privilege. Looking in the mirror may reveal physical changes: a more fragile appearance with wrinkles, graying hair, and maybe even a shorter stature. Beneath that appearance, there is a person with a determined resilience. As survivors of many life experiences, we make every effort to accept and adapt to our physical limitations and quietly cope with our aches and pains. With the blessing of years, we recognize our mistakes and shortcomings. We are talented at improvising and our creativity far surpasses our limitations. Guided by a spiritual quest, we rely on our faith to find serenity and peace.

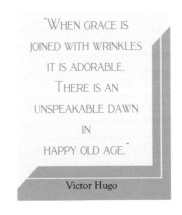

"When grace is joined with wrinkles it is adorable. There is an unspeakable dawn in happy old age."

Victor Hugo

Friendships are one of our greatest assets in the evening of our lives. As we live into our senior years, we have the time to enjoy reminiscing with friends who share similar life experiences. No matter how difficult the hardships of our youth, it is heartening to share the fond memories of the *"good old days."*

The older years announce the need for an extra push getting out of a chair, caution on the stairs, knowing it is officially time to stay off ladders and say no to high heels. With age comes the mourning of loved ones who have gone before us. Our hearts ache as we regroup to celebrate and cherish their memories. Counting our blessings becomes our focus. As we learn the art of letting go, we discover less is more, and life is a precious commodity. This earthly journey has an end, but the wisdom of years tells us to stay present and celebrate today's blessings. Our tomorrows are in God's hands.

Among the struggles of aging gracefully is memory loss. Forgetfulness and other physical limitations cause side effects. It is not uncommon for the elderly to experience brain fog, lower energy, and worry about the future. Physical exercise at any age is a positive approach to holistic health. We seek the energy to keep going and strive to be as active as possible. The gift of living and doing according to our body's internal sensors is the most remarkable grace. It is essential to take gentle care of ourselves and to seek balance with moderation. *Aging with grace* is not for the faint-hearted. Accepting the slowing down process is not easy. The most gracious among us strive to be peacemakers, living in the present with a grateful heart. Amazingly, we adapt well to the effects of aging, always finding a good reason to celebrate the gift of life.

With the *gift of time*, giving back seems right and very rewarding. We pray for the grace to see more clearly and love more tenderly. The aging process has taught us to stay calm during a crisis and to understand rather than judge. On a positive note, we now have the time to do the things we have put off for years: read books, go to movies, have a leisurely lunch with a friend, and check our bucket list and say, *"Why Not?"* Our mature perspective reminds us that the days of impressing others are over. Titles, accomplishments, and degrees do not define us. We strive to live by grace, not by perfection. It is a joy to take the time to smell the flowers and embrace all we are as we continue to grow in wisdom, age, and grace. Enjoy the blessings of this day!

Ponder this thought: *"The afternoon knows what the morning never suspected."*

Robert Frost

JUST FOR TODAY...

Date: _____

Journaling...

Being YOU Is Enough

It is easy to compare yourself to others and perceive them as being better than you. What is observed in others usually does not reveal their complexities. It is common to have a public persona that screens out the private matters of our hearts and gives the message that all is well. No matter how we feel or what burdens we carry, we shield others from knowing our struggles. In subtle ways, we have become masters at the art of hiding behind an invisible mask to conceal our feelings, playing the game of pretending. Unlike wearing a protective covering to limit the spread of COVID-19, our invisible mask protects us from revealing the hurts that weigh heavy on our hearts. We work hard at projecting a positive image, believing we are not quite good enough. The belief we are less than is embedded in our psyche and difficult to erase. Understanding the source of our self-doubts helps us to let go of our-emotional pain. We all have a fundamental need to love and to be loved. It is a universal longing. We do not want to disappoint because being rejected is so painful.

" You may not control all the events that happen to you. But you can decide not to be reduced by them. "

Maya Angelou

Slowly, wake up the true you underneath the pretense and camouflage. It is a welcomed relief to feel safe enough to remove the invisible mask. Embrace the person you have come to know and understand, the person with strengths and weaknesses. Believe in your goodness, your uniqueness, and your special qualities. Avoid negative self-talk and comparing yourself with others. Your happiness increases as you explore the many facets of yourself that affirm your authenticity. Love and honor the experiences that shaped you. Don't let the ugliness in others degrade the beauty within you. You count! You are a gift to our world. Once you come to appreciate who you are, you will begin living in peaceful harmony.

You may be frustrated with your limitations, faults, and circumstances, some beyond your control. What you think you need and want may not be what will bring you happiness. Happiness is finding contentment with who you are. WHAT MAKES YOU A BLESSING TO OTHERS? WHAT ARE THE QUALITIES THAT MAKE YOU SPECIAL? Being you is enough but not an excuse to stop becoming. Every day is a new beginning and a new opportunity to participate in *the art of becoming*. Your lived experiences mold your outlook, challenging you to expand your horizon and chase after your dreams.

Humbly accept the compliments that come your way. They are a true reflection of your authentic self. Your peers are your best and honest critics. Start each day by being true to yourself. Take off the mask you have been hiding behind and expose the real you, with all your flaws and imperfections. More importantly, believe in your goodness. Accept others the way you wish to be accepted. Don't judge or reject them based on what you perceive to be their limitations; instead, take the time to find their unique qualities. Above all else, strive to find your inner peace.

Steve Jobs reminds us, *"Our time is limited. So, don't waste it living someone else's life."* Instead, embrace who you are and pray for the courage to let go of who you are not. Happiness is not always having the best, rather making the best of everything and every situation. When everything is crashing down around you, breathe and take care of the most important part of your world, YOU. And, when life shines an abundance of light on you, help light the path of those walking in darkness. We journey together, and together, we lift up each other.

Ponder this thought: *"Be yourself; everyone else is already taken."*

 Oscar Wilde

Just for Today...

Date: _____

Journaling...

Be Hopeful

DO YOU HAVE THE

courage

TO BRING FORTH THE

treasures

THAT ARE HIDDEN

within you?

Elizabeth Gilbert

COURAGE TO RISK AND TAKE CHANCES

Scott Peck reminds us, *"Life is difficult."* In his book, *"The Road Less Traveled,"* he shares that life's challenges can either make or break us. It takes courage to live in the shades of difficult times, not knowing how long they will last or what the outcomes will be. The unknowns are what paralyze us from feeling hopeful. At the day's end, we are often surprised by the unexpected happenings that crept into our twenty-four-hour day. With amazement and courage, we stepped up to the plate and responded appropriately.

The word *"courage"* has roots in old French *Coeur ("heart")*, from the Latin word for heart, *cor*. Having courage means moving from the heart to do what is right, despite fear or potential danger. Our heart knows the truth and what we need to do to act justly and to love tenderly.

The COVID-19 pandemic has taught us many lessons about courage and survivorship. As survivors of many near catastrophes, we can put up with almost anything, at least for a while. It takes courage to stay positive during a trying time. Living through challenging situations can build character, teach patience, and broaden our perspective on our lives' priorities. Taking it a day, even a minute at a time, helps prioritize things and cope with disappointments and losses. Living through challenging times takes courage and confirms the belief that we can survive and even thrive as we discover the depth of our resilience.

A few years after I survived advanced-stage ovarian cancer, I was restless and confused. I didn't know how I wanted to spend the rest of my life. I was floundering and searching for what, I was not sure. At the medical center where I received my chemotherapy and had my surgeries, a staff nurse told me about an

Outward Bound program in Colorado for cancer survivors. A few weeks later, I was on a plane to Colorado to risk and stretch my limits with the hope of discovering a new horizon. I was in uncharted territory with no idea of what was about to take place. It took courage to show up a thousand miles from home, in a strange place, to spend time with cancer survivors that I had never met. During the flight, I questioned why I was opting to risk again after taking so many risks. I realized I was on a quest to understand myself. It was humbling and empowering, and the reward of risking filled me with new hope. Until tested, we never know the depth of our resilience.

"COURAGE DOESN'T ALWAYS ROAR. SOMETIMES COURAGE IS THE QUIET VOICE AT THE END OF THE DAY SAYING I WILL TRY AGAIN TOMORROW."

Mary Anne Radmacher

It is to your advantage to find comfort in your vulnerability and your fear of risk-taking. It is rewarding to be decisive about your goals and chart a course to attain them. WHAT IS THE CHALLENGE WORTH TO YOU? There is no guarantee what you are undertaking will be successful. You may fail and may discover you are not in control of a lot of things. However, when the risk pays off and you accomplish your goal, you become more resilient and confident. Although it can be scary, it is also exciting. Faith and hope go together. Risk usually implies change. You risk because you are restless and see the need for change. Change is a fact of life, and change means things will be different – to what extent, you don't know.

I don't believe we are searching for a perfect life, just a more meaningful one where the ordinary greets the extraordinary and we rejoice with surprise. In all things, strive to seek the truth of who you are. You are courageous and will rise to do the unbelievable when necessary. Remember, you are capable of amazing things.

Ponder this thought: *"Every adversity brings new experiences and new lessons."*

 Lailah Gift Akita

JUST FOR TODAY...

Date: _____

Journaling...

Be Hopeful

DARE TO DREAM

When you dare to dream and believe in yourself, you will be surprised as you surpass your expectations. Don't be afraid to reach for the stars. Deal with your deepest fears. Often, the feeling of inadequacy is the fear that cripples and prevents you from succeeding. With God's grace and the support of others, you have all it takes to dare and to believe in yourself and your dreams. Daring involves stepping out of your comfort zone and making the commitment to hard work.

HAVE YOU EVER BEEN TOLD YOU HAVE A GIFT, A SPECIAL TALENT? Believe what those close to you tell you. They have a good insight into your talents and abilities. You need to believe and dare to risk to reach your goal. Doubting your abilities is a huge block to success. Begin the hard work of accomplishing your goal. Remember, it is a huge commitment, and the road will not be easy. Failures, frustrations, disappointments, and roadblocks will cause you to doubt, but give it time. Sometimes it is easier to give up instead of accepting the challenge and giving it your all. Let go of your doubt and trust in your God-given talents. Commit to DARE to DREAM and take the first step to have your dream come true. It is never too late to begin a new adventure. Don't let age be your disqualifier. Regardless of age, if you can dream it, most of the time, you can achieve it. Unearth your dreams of years ago and pursue them. You now have the time.

Another aspect of dreaming is daring to empower yourself and others by speaking up without fearing rejection or ridicule. When you dare to believe in yourself by lifting your voice, you are on your way to becoming a better version of yourself. You never know what your testimony does to inspire others. You never know who you are helping by having the courage to speak your truth. Silence is not the answer.

Marianne Williamson reminds us, *"As we let our light shine, we unconsciously permit other people to do the same. As we are liberated from our fear, our presence liberates others."* Your resilience will steer you in the right direction. Dare to believe in yourself because others are waiting for permission from you to let their light shine.

As you walk into the future, have courage and believe your future holds endless possibilities. Try to overcome the fear and self-doubt and work toward building your self-confidence and self-esteem. Believe you are talented and use your gifts for the good of yourself and others. Be proactive in achieving your goal. It takes hard work and commitment to stay enthusiastic and focused. Hold on to the expectation that what you want will happen, and daily commit to it.

Believe in yourself because not walking in your purpose is too great a mistake to make when you have so much to offer this world. For example, the little boy in the picture has big dreams of becoming a firefighter. He dresses the part and role-plays in his dreams. Children dream dreams, and grownups believe their childhood dreams will come true.

> "THIS WORLD IS
> VAST ENOUGH
> TO HANDLE
> ANYTHING
> YOU DARE
> TO DREAM."
>
> Hill Harper

Keep going even when the going gets tough. Focus on your goal to accomplish your dreams and give it your very best. Success doesn't happen overnight. Sometimes it takes years of trying. The journey to the destination is at least as important as the destination itself. Your life's journey is about living every day with a sense of meaning and contentment. Try to live in the present and celebrate the little milestones along your way.

Ponder this thought: *"Patience is not passive waiting. Patience is active acceptance of the process required to attain your goals and dreams."*

Ray A. Davis

JUST FOR TODAY...

Date: _____

Journaling...

Be Hopeful

Empathy

Empathy: Tenderness Felt and Expressed

Learning to stand in somebody else's shoes, to see through their eyes, is how a bond of trust develops. People notice how much you care more than how much you know. Leo Buscaglia shares a good insight, *"Too often, we underestimate the power of a touch, a smile, a kind word, a listening ear, an honest compliment, or the smallest act of caring."* Empathy is the ability to imagine what someone else is feeling or what it's like to be in their situation. Empathy is a quality that allows us to feel the hurt or pain of another as if it were our pain. Being empathic is a way of being one with another in their pain.

"I THINK WE ALL HAVE EMPATHY. WE MAY NOT HAVE ENOUGH COURAGE TO DISPLAY IT."

Maya Angelou

If you have a good insight into the feelings another is experiencing, you can understand their emotions and struggles as if they were your own. You know, and you take notice. No explanation is necessary for you to comprehend what another is experiencing. Being empathic is also being compassionate. If you are compassionate and empathic, you are a gift when someone needs to be understood and loved. Many people seem fine on the exterior but are carrying heavy emotional burdens and feeling deep anguish inside. The empathic person can see beneath the surface and resonate with another's emotional pain.

Your emotional challenges empower you with an understanding to respond empathically to the struggles of others. Going through a difficult time can deplete your energy and cause you to feel depressed and overwhelmed. Try to focus on good coping skills, seek out friends and professional help to guide you to transcend the hurt and process the heartache. Your life will be richer, and you will be more sensitive to the pain of others because of your journey through challenging times.

Your empathic nature is a source of healing to others. It is a special gift to be able to listen empathically without judgment. Your hurting friends need someone to understand their pain and be with them in the rawness of their agony. They do not want you to solve their problem but need you to be emotionally supportive during the darkness of their struggle. They need the assurance that you care and that better days are ahead. An understanding friend can be a lifesaver in troubled times. Don't shy away when your friend is brokenhearted. Reach out with loving kindness, let your friend know you care, and you will not abandon him during a struggling time.

Qualities of an empathic person include being vulnerable and listening intensely to the spoken words and, more importantly, to the *unspoken words*. Avoid making assumptions and withhold judgments. Instead, show you deeply care by your gentle and prayerful presence. In a time of need, an empathetic person can save a life.

Empathy is tender-heartedness felt and expressed. To be empathic is to look into another's eyes and know that what you see in the hurting person is only bruised but not broken. Understanding the role of wholeness, wellness, and healing can help mend their hurt and anxious feelings.

Empathy strengthens our resolve to reach out to strangers when they are in crisis. Former President Barack Obama said, *"The biggest deficit that we have in our society and in the world right now is an empathy deficit. We are in great need of people being able to stand in somebody else's shoes and see the world through their eyes."* HOW DO YOU HELP FILL THE EMPATHY DEFICIT IN OUR WOUNDED SOCIETY?

Ponder this thought: *"First of all, if you learn a simple trick, Scout, you'll get along a lot better with all kinds of folks. You never really understand a person until you consider things from his point of view . . . until you climb into his skin and walk around in it."*

Atticus, *"To Kill A Mockingbird"*

JUST FOR TODAY...

Date: _____

Journaling...

Be Hopeful

friendship...

a precious gift

Friendship: A Precious Gift

To have a good friend is the gift of a lifetime. A special friend shares a bond with you that is a blessing beyond measure. Time and distance do not diminish the bond that seals your friendship. As the song reminds us: *"People who need people are the luckiest people in the world."* There is a mystery that draws two people to each other as special friends. Friendship is a relationship of mutual affection.

A special friend knows you inside and out, knows what you love and what you fear, your deepest secrets, pains, mistakes, failures, and dreams. You feel safe knowing your friend has your best interests at heart. In the presence of your friend, you can be yourself. You do not have to pretend you are okay when you are not. A friend is there to celebrate your good news, rejoices with you when you are happy, and is by your side when you are hurting or sad. There are no limitations to how a friend will support you. A friend will pray for you and with you, knowing when to talk and when to be silent. A dear friend is always honest with you, does not mince words, and always has your back, helping you shine in your best light. A friend shows respect, honors your uniqueness, and tolerates your idiosyncrasies.

When you feel lost and scared, your friend is there as a sounding board, not judging but understanding. When you need someone who cares, your friend is there. When all is right with your world, your friend shares your peacefulness. Your friend is your confidant, the person who loves you unconditionally and stands by you through thick and thin. A true friend challenges you to be a better person. The beauty of a shared friendship is its reciprocity.

Being a special friend means you are compassionate and caring. A friend stands by you even when others doubt you and is not worried about losing popularity because of you. That friend will drop everything to be by your side.

Your friend has the uncanny ability to read your mind before you speak. Just by exchanging a glance, you each know precisely what the other is thinking. A friend does not betray your confidence, does not judge you, but understands *"why"* even before you know *"why."* Your friend cheers you on and stands by your side when you struggle and celebrates with you in good times. A friend does not try to outdo you, does not act superior. There is no competition; rather gratitude for shared experiences. A friend gives without expecting anything in return. We have many acquaintances in life, but a loyal friend is a treasure to cherish.

God puts friends in our lives at the right time to guide us on our journeys. They help us find our rhythm and lighten our steps. Valued and loved and much appreciated, sometimes they are meant to journey with us for just a while and then part, leaving an imprint on our hearts forever.

It is a special blessing when two childhood friends can continue to share their friendship into adulthood and senior years. It is a joy for old friends to reminisce about the precious memories of their past, laugh about the silly times, close calls, failed romances, crazy incidents that were so important at the time.

The poem by Samantha Glovier describes the blessing of being a true friend. *"A true friend is someone who will always be there when a friend is in need. A true friend will see the things you see and never disrespect you for what you believe."* Friendship is a precious gift.

Ponder this thought: *"Friendship is always a sweet responsibility, never an opportunity."*

Khalil Gibran

JUST FOR TODAY...

Date: _____

Journaling...

Be Hopeful

The pain
of an
aching heart

GRIEF: THE PAIN OF AN ACHING HEART

Going through a difficult loss: the death of a loved one, a breakup, a divorce, the loss of a job - is devastating. Each kind of loss has its heartache that can cripple you emotionally. Yes, life is complicated, and grieving a loss is emotionally taxing. Some losses are more complicated than others. It is a painful reality that makes you question *"why."* Sometimes you do not know where to turn to find solace, to seek healing. No insurance policy can protect you from getting sick or suffering a broken heart. It may provide the care you need when ill and help pay for psychotherapy when your heart aches, but it provides no immunity. WHERE DO YOU BEGIN TO FIND HOPE?

"GRIEF NEVER ENDS. BUT IT CHANGES. IT IS A PASSAGE. NOT A PLACE TO STAY. GRIEF IS NOT A SIGN OF WEAKNESS NOR A LACK OF FAITH. IT IS THE PRICE OF LOVE."

Anonymous

If you feel sad, depressed, or anxious because of a loss, please know that these are painful and real symptoms of grieving. It takes time to recover from any loss. A significant loss can seem impossible to recover from when the tugs at your heartstrings are so powerful. Yet, as unbelievable as it may seem, the human spirit is resilient. The grieving process takes time, and that timeline is unique to each person and every situation. A colleague and friend, Paul Tschudi, refers to loss as a life transition. *"In order to have a new beginning, you have to let go of something...It is about letting go of that which was and preparing for that which is to come – a normal and natural part of life. Perhaps it makes us more fully human."* To mourn a loss is a way to ease the grief that grips your entire being. Mourning is an essential step in processing your loss. While the pain lessens over time, coping with all the symptoms is a lifetime task. Sometimes the loss seems very unreal. At times it feels very distant, and at other times it feels like yesterday. Your memories are reminders of what once was. As you grieve, you may find yourself avoiding friends and social engagements. Remember: there is no right or wrong way to grieve. Your way is the right way for you. Let your heart lead you as you live through the rawness of your loss. C. S. Lewis shares, *"Grief is like a long valley, a winding valley where any bend may reveal a totally new landscape."* You cannot predict what you will experience as you work through the emotional ups and downs that are normal during the grieving process.

As a society, we find ways to deny the finality of death. We have adopted the word *"passed"* to replace the word *"died."* As difficult as it is, we need to find a way to gradually process the loss so we can accept the reality that our loved one has died. It is a big step toward finding peace. There are degrees of loss, and there are situations that cause multiple losses, some happening simultaneously. Living through loss while struggling to make sense of it is challenging. While grieving, it is important to take gentle care, lower expectations, and give ourselves the time to do the things we need to do. It is okay not to be okay. There are no rules. Although your pain is very raw at first, one day, you will wake up to a better day. Until then, be good to yourself.

After a significant loss, it is possible to experience a broken heart and feel the physical and emotional pain of *"broken heart syndrome"* that can mimic heart attack symptoms. The immeasurable and devastating blow of grief is complicated and shakes us to our core. Mending a broken heart is a lengthy process. Finding the path to healing is finding a way from brokenness to wholeness. Memories once painful help fashion the potential for tomorrow's peace and contentment.

Ponder this thought: *"They whom we love and lose are no longer where they were before. They are now wherever we are."*

St. John Chrysostom

JUST FOR TODAY...

Date: _____

Journaling...

Be Hopeful

"Take off your sandals,

for the place

where you are standing

is

HOLY."

Exodus 3:5

HOLY GROUND: WHAT WE RENDER SACRED

WHAT DO YOU RENDER SACRED? WHERE IS YOUR HOLY GROUND? When you stand on holy ground, you are at a sacred place that transcends your fears and helps you feel peaceful and less anxious. Your homes can be sanctuaries of hallowed ground that anchor you. God accompanies you on your daily journey and walks with you during the challenging moments of your life.

You stand on holy ground when you:

"To touch the soul of another human being is to walk on holy ground."

Stephen Covey

- ❧ are on the same wavelength as our soulmate.
- ❧ are alone but not lonely.
- ❧ come into the presence of God while being in the presence of another.
- ❧ see the glory of God in the rising and setting of the sun.
- ❧ know and feel the presence of God in the ordinary.
- ❧ reminisce about the special times.
- ❧ feel the anguish of another and stay in their company to help console and heal.

Yes, you are living on holy ground and God is with you every step of the way. K. J. Ramsey offers encouragement: *"Be gentle toward all that remains unhealed and unfinished in you. The space between today's hurt and tomorrow's healing is sacred ground."* Pause to recognize the sacred surrounding you. Be an instrument of God's loving peace as you walk through your day. Be the encouraging voice, the quiet smile, the loving heart that sees the sacred in the happenings of your day. And, as you close your eyes at night, thank God for being able to tread on holy ground and for the gift of seeing the sacred surrounding you. *"Remove the sandals from your feet, for the place where you are standing is holy ground." Exodus 3:5.*

Holy Ground
Alethea Kehas

I'M NOT GOING TO TELL YOU THAT THE MOON KEEPS THE SECRETS OF THE TIDES
BECAUSE YOU HOLD THE OCEAN IN YOUR BODY.
WHEN YOU ARE STILL, FEEL THE WAVES RUSHING YOU SOFTLY TO THE EDGES,
BRINGING YOU BACK TO CENTER.
YOU WERE NOT BORN BROKEN AND FORGOTTEN
YOU WERE BIRTHED WITH THE STRENGTH OF COHESION
AND THE FORCE OF A DIVISION THAT REMEMBERS UNITY.
ONE THOUSAND LIVES MIGHT BRING YOU BACK TO THE PLACE OF ORIGIN
OR YOU CAN GO THERE NOW,
RIDING THE BREATH LIKE A WAVE
TO SEED THE SACRED WITHIN YOUR BODY BECOMING THE HOLY GROUND
FERTILE TO THE QUICKENING PULSE, RIPE WITH LIFE,
IT ROCKS WITH THE MEMORY OF HOME.

Ponder this thought: *"Be patient with yourself. Self-growth is tender; it's holy ground. There's no greater investment."*

Stephen Covey

- 36 -

JUST FOR TODAY...

Date: _____

Journaling...

Be Hopeful

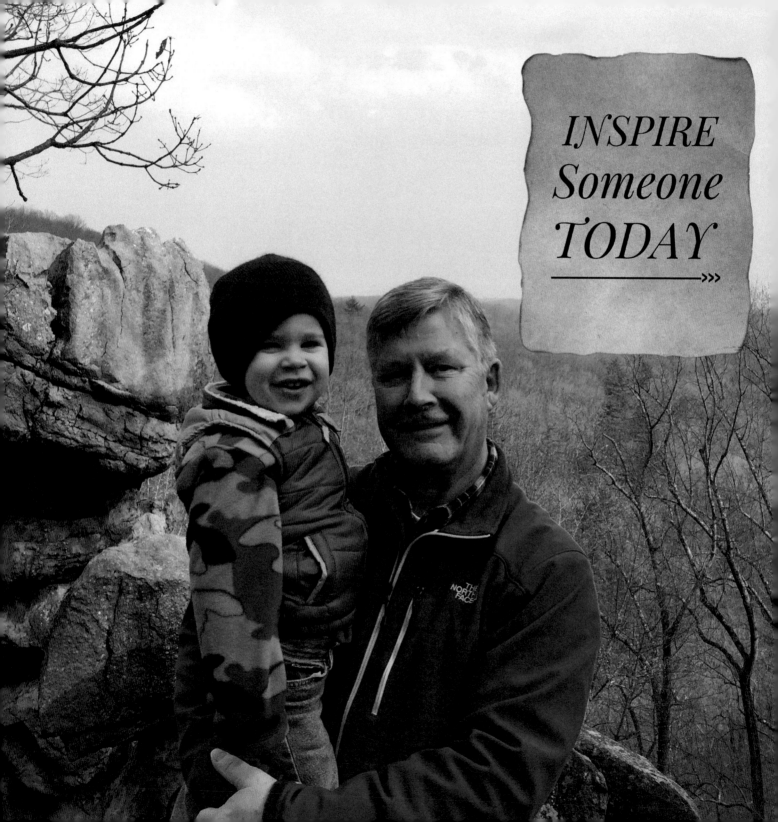

INSPIRE
Someone
TODAY

Inspire Someone Today: Be a Mentor

Taking the time to notice a young person's potential and encouraging that gift can forever change the direction of their life. It can open the door to unimagined possibilities. Mentoring is reaching out to recognize the unique talent of another and working to help advance their ability. Mentors are people who can support, advise, and guide others. Mentoring means taking a particular interest in another and nurturing that person as they begin to focus and commit their time and energy to perfect an innate talent. Mentoring is a gift that empowers. It is a positive way to give back and to experience joy in empowering another. It is rewarding to know your interest and effort changed another and infused a feeling of hope that was the incentive for success.

"THE GREATEST GOOD YOU CAN DO FOR ANOTHER IS NOT JUST TO SHARE YOUR RICHES BUT TO REVEAL TO HIM HIS OWN."

Benjamin Disraeli

As caring adults, we give and receive informal mentoring every day. In his book, *Shared Wisdom: The Practical Art of Giving and Receiving Mentoring*, Dr. Robert Wicks offers us the opportunity to make the most of these natural encounters. He states that a mentor is a *"beautiful part of adult life...noting not to mentor is to miss one of the most rewarding experiences available: the imparting and receiving of life's wisdom."*

What does it take to be a mentor? It takes a person who has a caring heart and a passion for affirming the goodness of others. Whether you are a mentor or a mentee, the art of mentoring establishes a special bond. The benefits of mentoring are myriad. Mentoring can be immensely rewarding for both mentor and mentee, providing many opportunities to learn, share, and gain new insights. Mentoring involves working in a trusted relationship and overcoming roadblocks encountered, including the ups and downs. Good mentors have patience, enthusiasm, and a genuine desire to walk with their mentees through uncertain times. The mentor is available when obstacles seem overwhelming, offering support and guidance. Endearing relationships are born from co-journeying through the highs and lows of mentoring. The reward comes when the mentee marks a milestone and is happy and content with their accomplishment. The greatest blessing is staying in touch and sharing the good realized by your coaching and support. A mentor's gift is seeing others flourish and make a positive contribution to society.

Mentoring is a beautiful way of both giving back and paying forward. Grandparents are the epitome of dedicated mentors. Their unconditional love and direction are invaluable in guiding their grandchildren. The gift of mentoring does not need to diminish as you get older. You are constantly transitioning, evaluating choices, and exploring ever-changing trends in your lives. You can mentor same-age friends as they are reevaluating their choices and options in their senior years. Mentoring usually focuses on sharing your gift of time, helping others bypass pitfalls as they choose to live a meaningful life. You will feel a sense of purpose when you share your lessons learned and the wisdom of your years. Consider sharing your gift of mentoring to inspire and make a positive difference in another's life. Your volunteer time and caring spirit will prove to be a blessing.

Ponder this thought: *"I've learned that people will forget what you said, people will forget what you did, but people will never forget how you made them feel."*

Maya Angelou

JUST FOR TODAY...

Date: _____

Journaling...

Be Hopeful

JOY OF PAYING IT FORWARD

Paying it forward is doing something kind for someone after another person did something kind for you. The joy of paying it forward is that you do something for someone you do not know, not as payback, but as a kind act, expecting nothing in return. Sometimes this creates a chain reaction, and the recipient of your kindness passes it on to another. You don't have to be rich, powerful, or influential to pay it forward. For example, you can volunteer your time to help with the needs of the less fortunate in your community. or visit the elderly and offer to assist them with little chores. Being aware of and responding to the needs of others spreads joy and makes you an instrument of God's healing love.

"WE MAKE A LIVING BY WHAT WE GET. WE MAKE A LIFE BY WHAT WE GIVE."

Winston S. Churchill

Doing a good deed for an unsuspecting stranger is a beautiful and selfless act. Not only will it remind the person that generosity and kindness still exist in the world, but it will also encourage the benefactor to be kind and compassionate to others. Life provides many opportunities to pay it forward. All you have to do is be attentive to the possibilities. Reach beyond your circle of family, friends, and acquaintances to consider strangers as recipients of your good deeds. The greatest gift is in giving freely without expecting anything in return. Even a small act of giving brings joy to another. Sometimes, our world needs a little inspiration to change people's lives and encourage them to do good to others. There are so many little ways to show you care. Reach out! It will warm your heart and the hearts of others. At the end of the day, you will realize how little you need, how much you have, and the value of the human connection. Pay it forward. You will not regret it.

A Kaleidoscope of Ways to Pay It Forward

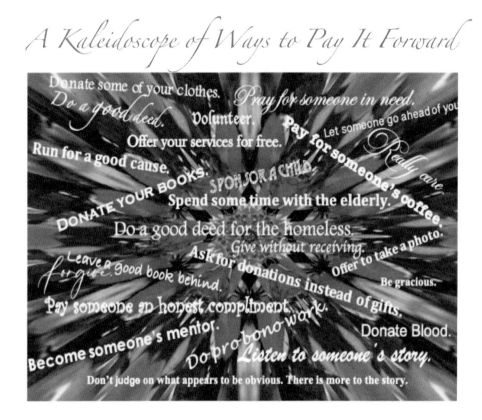

Donate some of your clothes. Pray for someone in need.
Do a good deed. Volunteer. Pay for someone's coffee.
Offer your services for free. Let someone go ahead of you.
Run for a good cause. Really care.
DONATE YOUR BOOKS. SPONSOR A CHILD.
Spend some time with the elderly.
Do a good deed for the homeless.
Give without receiving.
Leave a good book behind. Ask for donations instead of gifts. Offer to take a photo.
forgive. Be gracious.
Pay someone an honest compliment.
Become someone's mentor. Do pro bono work. Donate Blood.
Listen to someone's story.
Don't judge on what appears to be obvious. There is more to the story.

Ponder this thought: *"You may be only one person in this world, but to one person at one time, you are the world."*

 Anonymous

JUST FOR TODAY...

Date: _____

Journaling...

Be Hopeful

Kind-Heartedness

Being kind-hearted is a gracious way to bring joy into others' lives and add meaning to your own. Being kind allows you to communicate better, be more compassionate, and be a positive force for good. Kindness has its trustworthy source deep within you, and while some people are innately kind, kindness is something everyone can learn. The definition of kind-hearted is having or showing a sympathetic or empathic nature. Kindness begets kindness.

Kindness reflects deep caring for all beings. Practice kindness and generosity toward others. Genuine acts of kindness expect nothing, come with no strings attached, and place no conditions on anything done or said. Begin by being kind to yourself. Cultivate kindness for the good of your health. Kindness promotes a sense of well-being that improves your mental state. Be kind to everyone, not only those close to you. Be a good listener. Listen with your heart. Make the time to pay attention to what is shared as well as what is not shared. Resting at the heart of kindness are happiness, joy, and gratitude. You will see the good in others and the world, restoring your sense of faith in humanity. Be friendly. Give compliments when they are sincere. Practice random acts of kindness.

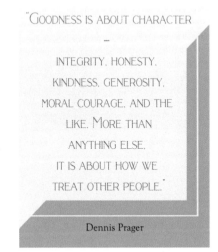

"GOODNESS IS ABOUT CHARACTER — INTEGRITY, HONESTY, KINDNESS, GENEROSITY, MORAL COURAGE, AND THE LIKE. MORE THAN ANYTHING ELSE, IT IS ABOUT HOW WE TREAT OTHER PEOPLE."

Dennis Prager

When you are kind to others, you are also kind to yourself. William Arthur Ward reminds us, *"a warm smile is the universal language of kindness."* Kindness begins with the understanding that we all struggle.

There are countless ways of showing kindness. The illustration below suggests random acts of kindness for you to consider. When you act with kind-heartedness, you respond from the goodness of your heart and touch the heart of another.

ACTS OF KINDNESS

A "THINKING OF YOU" NOTE *a smile*

A PRAYER   A KIND WORD   AN INVITE

A walk together   A "check in" phone call

A GENTLE TOUCH

a helpful hand   *A listening ear*

AN AFFIRMING TEXT MESSAGE

A nod of approval   A SPECIAL SURPRISE

a bottle of wine   *An "I care" message*

a little " You are Special" gift

A LOVING HUG   A KIND HEART

a thoughtful gesture

Ponder this thought: *"Every word that conveys altruism, amiability, consideration, helpfulness, care or concern has no meaning unless it is followed by a genuine and graceful action devoid of expecting something in return."*

Freddy J. W. Parker

JUST FOR TODAY...

Date: _____

Journaling...

Be Hopeful

LOVE TENDERLY

St. John of the Cross reminds us, *"At the end of life, we are going to be judged based on our love for one another."* Mother Teresa lived the words of St. John of the Cross and made it her mission to extend loving kindness to poor, sick, dying, or marginalized people. To love and be loved is what life is all about. To love is much more than sharing special moments and joyful times. It is about being a supportive presence in good and challenging times. When you love tenderly, you love with great sensitivity to the needs and wants of others. You don't count the cost. Reaching out in love is an expression of intimacy, a connection built on trust and friendship.

In 1965, *"What the World Needs Now is Love,"* with lyrics by Hal David and music by Burt Bacharach, became a popular song. The refrain's last line has a timeless message: *"Love is not just for some, but for everyone"* echoes our heart's desire. We celebrate and affirm all loving relationships and admire the remarkable bond that unites those who love.

"WHAT THE WORLD NEEDS NOW IS LOVE, SWEET LOVE
IT'S THE ONLY THING THAT THERE'S JUST TOO LITTLE OF
WHAT THE WORLD NEEDS NOW IS LOVE, SWEET LOVE
NO, NOT JUST FOR SOME BUT FOR EVERYONE."

Fall in Love

WHAT YOU ARE IN LOVE WITH
WHAT SEIZES YOUR IMAGINATION
WILL AFFECT EVERYTHING.
IT WILL DECIDE WHAT WILL GET YOU OUT OF BED IN THE MORNING.
WHAT YOU DO WITH YOUR EVENINGS.
HOW YOU SPEND YOUR WEEKENDS.
WHAT YOU READ.
WHO YOU KNOW.
WHAT BREAKS YOUR HEART.
AND WHAT AMAZES YOU WITH JOY AND GRATITUDE.

FALL IN LOVE,
STAY IN LOVE,
AND IT WILL DECIDE EVERYTHING.

Attributed to Fr. Pedro Arrupe, SJ (1907-1991)

Life is short. NOW is the time to give yourself permission to love and be loved and feel the intimacy of that life-sharing, life-saving connection.

Ponder this thought: *"Being unwanted, unloved, uncared for, forgotten by everybody, I think is a much greater hunger, a much greater poverty than the person who has nothing to eat."*

St. Teresa of Calcutta

JUST FOR TODAY...

Date: _____

Journaling...

Be Hopeful

MISSING SOMEONE SPECIAL

D O YOU EVER JUST GET WAVES OF MISSING SOMEONE? DO YOU GO FOR A WHILE AND FEEL OKAY, AND THEN ALL OF A SUDDEN, YOUR HEART ACHES? Missing someone is your heart's way of reminding you that you love someone special. When you lose someone you love, it takes time to shift from living without them to living with the love they left behind.

My dear sister, Ann, died after a long battle with cancer. Her diagnosis devastated me. I had lost other loved ones, but the thought of losing Ann seemed unbearable. She was more than a sister to me. Ann was my best friend, my confidant, my cheerleader, and my role model. Ann and I shared a special bond that united us in a relationship of mutual love. Ann was affectionately called *"Ladybugs."* Tiny ladybugs appear on the journaling pages as a way of honoring memories of a very special lady, my sister, Ann.

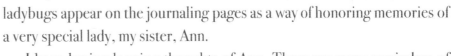

"THOSE WE LOVE AND LOSE ARE ALWAYS CONNECTED BY HEARTSTRINGS INTO INFINITY."

Terri Guillemets

I keep having longing thoughts of Ann. There are many reminders of her all around me. For the first year after Ann's death, I unconsciously craved her favorite foods, wore the clothes she particularly liked, and tried to adopt her music and crafts style. I wanted to have vivid dreams of her, fearing I would forget her unique qualities. The passage of time helped me live with the reality that my sister is now with God. Remembering Ann often brings tears to my eyes, tears of love and gratitude for the blessing of having a wonderful sister in my life. Her spirit is very much alive in my heart.

Death is so final. Why does the separation hurt so much? We tend to do everything to hold on to memories. Yet, sad feelings linger in our grief. For months after a death, it is normal to question "*why.*"

In time, our prayer becomes one of gratitude for the gift of loving someone very special. The conversion from raw grief to acceptance happens when we can smile as memories of our loved one floods our thoughts. As we continue to heal, the heartache lessens, and we begin to refocus on cherishing the precious memories.

> "THERE IS A SACREDNESS IN TEARS. THEY ARE NOT THE MARK OF WEAKNESS, BUT OF POWER. THEY SPEAK MORE ELOQUENTLY THAN TEN THOUSAND TONGUES. THEY ARE THE MESSENGERS OF OVERWHELMING GRIEF, OF DEEP CONTRITION, AND OF UNSPEAKABLE LOVE."
>
> Washington Irving

Your life is forever changed when someone you love dies. Those that go before you will never again be part of your earthly journey. When you process your pain and grief, you can hold on to the memories that you hold dear. It is hard to live without someone who gave you so much to remember. Yet, there is a special strength revealed in growing through what you go through. As difficult as it is, it helps you to be compassionate to another's grieving heart.

The loss of a loved one walks beside you every day. The initial days of feeling the loss are like walking in a valley of tears. Heartache can be worse than any physical pain. The ache touches your soul and cries in inconsolable grief. It is unlike any other feeling. This hallowed place is the first and most difficult junction on the road to finding light, peace, and acceptance. Grieving offers no detour.

If you miss someone special today, take a break from your day and pause to remember the qualities you admired and loved about that person. Smile as you carry their cherished memories in the fullness of your heart.

Ponder this thought: *"Death leaves a heartache no one can heal; Love leaves a memory no one can steal."*

Mary Robinson

JUST FOR TODAY...

Date: _____

Journaling...

Be Hopeful

No Regrets?

As a hospice chaplain, I learned much about regret. I was surprised at how many of my patients got to the end of their lives, regretting the choices they made. They were remorseful about their broken relationships and unfulfilled dreams. Some had feelings of guilt and resentment that they never resolved. Many found the courage in their last days to ask for and offer forgiveness. My most profound moments were witnessing the peace and joy of love restored through acts of forgiveness. Their greatest regret was that they waited so long to seek forgiveness and mend broken relationships. It was beautiful to observe healed relationships. Seeing the joy of loved ones reconnected after a long and painful hiatus was heart-warming.

"Nobody gets to live life backward. Look ahead, that is where your future lies."

Ann Landers

More than likely, everyone will experience feelings of regret at least once in their lifetime. You can do several things to accept and overcome your guilt and shame so they do not restrict your *quality of life*. It is a blessing when remorse becomes a lesson learned. Do I have regrets? I do. Some were because of my poor choices; some were because of circumstances that negatively impacted my life, inflicting emotional suffering. I sought therapy to process my pain. My resolve has been to live a peaceful and happy life. We don't know how much time we have on this earth. Each day is a blessing filled with hope and promise. Forgiveness of self and others is a powerful healing agent. Shannon L. Alder imparts: *"One of the greatest regrets in life is being what others would want you to be, rather than being yourself."* Not wanting to hurt or disappoint others can keep us from sharing who we are and the desires of our hearts.

When I think about seeking peace, the *Serenity Prayer,* written by American theologian Reinhold Niebuhr, offers comfort and hope:

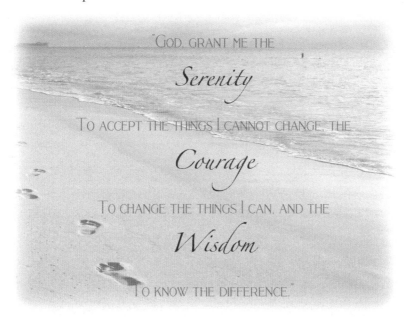

"GOD, GRANT ME THE

Serenity

TO ACCEPT THE THINGS I CANNOT CHANGE, THE

Courage

TO CHANGE THE THINGS I CAN, AND THE

Wisdom

TO KNOW THE DIFFERENCE."

Learn from your mistakes and believe you deserve a good life. Your past is history and does not have to enslave you with guilt for the rest of your life. Greet each new day with a positive attitude. Tread gently and seek a grateful heart. Let go of resentments and grudges. Forgive yourself and others. Be yourself. Your authentic self is your best self.

Ponder this thought: *"There is a strange comfort in knowing that no matter what happens today, the sun will rise again tomorrow."*

Aaron Lauritsen

Just for Today...

Date: _____

Journaling...

Be Hopeful

Be
Hopeful

Optimism: Finding Hope During Difficult Times

Having a hopeful attitude during a difficult time usually predicts a better outcome. Being optimistic helps you cope with the challenges that come your way. It helps you imagine affirmative results. A bright outlook gives you the energy to focus on the positive instead of dwelling on the harsh negatives. Optimism is an inclination to put a favorable outlook on actions and events, expecting a possible resolution. By being optimistic, you can aspire to imagine positive results and set aside the pessimistic predictions. A growing number of scientific studies suggest optimistic people tend to live longer and have better physical and mental health than those with a negative outlook.

All of my adult life, I have enjoyed the reputation of being positive. It is a gift that allows me to be optimistic and look to the brighter side, even in the darkest times. The word *"HOPE"* has been my mantra. Friends often tease me because my blood type is B Positive (B+), a good match for my positive attitude. I always believe there is a way things will work out. It may not be easy, but all will be well with creativity, ingenuity, and trust in God.

Hope plays a huge role in having a positive outlook on life. It gives you the motivation to change and live life fully. With hope in your heart, you can dream and believe in a better future. You can draw on your inner resilience and your conviction that your spirit of hopefulness will carry you forward. Finding hope helps you to draw on the positivity of affirming people, places, and things. Life does not have to be perfect to be beautiful. Strive for beauty. Appreciate the small moments of happiness that take you by surprise. Emily Dickinson's poem gives an image to *hope*, a word deeply felt but hard to describe:

Hope Is The Thing With Feathers

Emily Dickinson

"HOPE" IS THE THING WITH FEATHERS –
THAT PERCHES IN THE SOUL –
AND SINGS THE TUNE WITHOUT THE WORDS –
AND NEVER STOPS AT ALL –

THE SWEETEST – IN THE GALE – IS HEARD –
AND SORE MUST BE THE STORM –
THAT COULD ABASH THE LITTLE BIRD
THAT KEPT SO MANY WARM –

I'VE HEARD IT IN THE CHILLEST LAND –
AND ON THE STRANGEST SEA –
YET – NEVER – IN EXTREMITY,
IT ASKED A CRUMB – OF ME

Ponder this thought: *"Now I know in part; then I shall know fully, even as I am fully known. And now these three remain: faith, hope, and love; and the greatest of these is love."*

1 Corinthians 13:1

JUST FOR TODAY...

Date: _____

Journaling...

Be Hopeful

Persistence

Persistence: Never Give Up

D O YOU EVER FEEL YOU ARE AT A CROSSROADS IN YOUR LIFE WHERE YOU ARE COASTING AND LIVING WITH UNPLEASANT REALITIES BECAUSE YOU DON'T HAVE THE ENERGY OR WHEREWITHAL TO DO SOMETHING ABOUT IT? Sometimes it is much easier to accept the inevitable rather than tackle the hurdles of journeying on a path to a more meaningful, peaceful life. Initiating a change in your outlook, attitude, and behavior can be daunting, but the reward is priceless: your happiness.

IF YOU COULD REWRITE YOUR LIFE SCRIPT, WHAT WOULD IT REFLECT? Do not let complacency, fear, and uncertainty cripple you from caring enough about your happiness to take the next step and begin the journey to initiate positive change in your life.

"THE ONE WHO FALLS AND GETS UP IS STRONGER THAN THE ONE WHO NEVER TRIED. DO NOT FEAR FAILURE BUT RATHER FEAR NOT TRYING."

Roy T. Bennett

The time to act is now! Consider taking steps to make change happen instead of just wishing for it. Take the time to assess your situation and take responsibility for creating the desired change. Sometimes the change is more about your mental attitude than about a drastic lifestyle change. Pray for the wisdom to see more clearly what modifications in your life will generate peace and happiness. If necessary, seek professional and spiritual guidance to validate your goals and then work on a realistic plan to accomplish your life-altering dream. Walk with patience and confidence toward your goal. No one else can make choices for you, and no one should. It takes courage, patience, and perseverance to seek peace and contentment. Be persistent, investing the necessary time to establish your new reality. For example, your plan may be as simple as committing to meditation each day for ten minutes, deciding to leave a toxic or abusive relationship, or leaving a job that drains you of your dignity and self-worth.

You have to participate in the process of achieving your goal. The process doesn't happen automatically. The longer you persist, the more likely you will create the life you deserve. And, yes, you do deserve a wonderful life filled with happiness, joy, and peace.

Challenging times seem to be an expected happening in the unfolding mystery of life. Disappointments and tragic news might interrupt the normal rhythm of your life. Yet, even though the difficult times feel like they will break you, know you possess an incredible inner strength that can push you forward. Having the mindset to persist helps you to overcome your fears and doubts. While intentionally working toward a significant change, take gentle care of yourself. Take the time to quiet yourself. Jack Kornfield shares, *"Part of the art of quieting yourself is also to honor the tears that you carry."* Be persistent in finding gratitude for the blessings in your life. Every new day is a new beginning. Honor the tears of yesterday and look to this new day with a grateful heart. In the quiet of your being, decide what you can do today to improve your *quality of life*. Live today knowing God's grace accompanies you. Remember, you are stronger than you think, wiser than you believe, and more resilient than you ever imagined. Don't give up on your quest to seek a peaceful life.

WHAT CHANGES DO YOU WISH TO MAKE IN YOUR LIFE TO EXPERIENCE GREATER PEACE AND HAPPINESS?

Ponder this thought: *"You deserve a love that can conquer all, even the hardest temptations and the most unbearable discouragement. A love that can withstand the strongest and raging storms, you deserve the type of love that will keep you safe."*

Racquelshii Manuel

JUST FOR TODAY...

Date: _____

Journaling...

Quality of Life

Quality of life is about having satisfaction and living life to the fullest. It has to do with managing your health, well-being, and happiness and how these qualities become integrated with your spiritual and philosophical values. *Quality of life* is not just about the absence of disease but the intentionality of making every effort to live a good life every day.

IF LIFE WERE TO CHANGE DRAMATICALLY FOR YOU TODAY, WHAT WOULD YOU HOLD MOST DEAR? WHAT WOULD BE MOST IMPORTANT TO YOU?

Your life becomes richer when you challenge yourself to reflect on the choices you make, thoughts you think, and words you say. Sometimes you may forget you have something to offer others that only you can give. The more you can connect with our gifts,

> "THE REAL THINGS HAVEN'T CHANGED. IT IS STILL BEST TO BE HONEST AND TRUTHFUL; TO MAKE THE MOST OF WHAT WE HAVE; TO BE HAPPY WITH SIMPLE PLEASURES AND HAVE COURAGE WHEN THINGS GO WRONG."
>
> Laura Ingalls Wilder

talents, and qualities and let them shine, the better your life becomes. Your *quality of life* is about spreading your unique message, wisdom, and encouragement in whatever forms come to you. In these ways, you nurture and cultivate your relationships through your actions and words. You make investments in your relationships by listening, reaching out, and telling others you care. Cultivating depth in your relationships comes from being willing to learn from others, noting the unique value they offer, and expressing your gratitude.

Living your best *quality of life* means letting go of the small stuff, setting loving boundaries, showing empathy and understanding, giving selflessly to others, and reminding your family and friends how much you love and appreciate them.

Ask yourself, WHAT BRINGS ME JOY? AM I LIVING MY LIFE TO THE FULLEST? WHAT MAKES ME LAUGH? Humility is accepting who you are with your God-given talents and a realistic awareness of your abilities. The choices you make determine your *quality of life*. You can choose to celebrate and live a life filled with meaning by making choices that echo harmony and balance. To do so, you need to embrace all that you are and have a sense of purpose to live each day with a peaceful calmness.

Choosing to be healthy means following a protocol that improves your health. What you eat, when you sleep, when you exercise, when you pause to slow down and meditate, how you spend your free time – all of these are choices that affect your overall health and well-being. Moderation and balance help you avoid extremes. Taking time for yourself is not being selfish. It is giving you time to rejuvenate and replenish the reservoir of your energy.

Your best *quality of life* experience is your ability to look deep inside yourself and find the qualities needed to live your boldest dreams. *Quality of life* is about finding a happy balance. WILL YOU CHOOSE TO MAKE THE REST OF YOUR LIFE THE BEST OF YOUR LIFE, SHARING WARMTH, KINDNESS, AND COMPASSION, A LIFE THAT IS MEANINGFUL AND MORE PEACEFUL – HAPPIER? Pause! Enjoy life's simple pleasures.

Ponder this thought: *"In the end, it's not the years in your life that count. It's the life in your years."*

Abraham Lincoln

JUST FOR TODAY...

Date: _____

Journaling...

Be Hopeful

RESILIENCE

"BE STILL AND KNOW
I AM GOD." PSALM 46:10

RESILIENCE: ABILITY TO BOUNCE BACK

I often ponder our fragile yet resilient nature. How do we find the light amid uncertainty? I have seen people survive critical illnesses to resume a normal and active life. I have known others who have not survived a minor illness. I believe we have an innate fight within us to overcome obstacles. To me, resilience means finding a way through the frustration of what seems impossible. Resilience is the capacity to recover from difficulties and spring back.

Life presents you with many unexpected twists and turns - from everyday challenges of wonderful surprises to unexpected tragic events. The ability to adapt well to life-changing situations is, in part, thanks to your resilient spirit. Adverse events don't have to chart a course for the rest of your life. Becoming more resilient not only helps you through difficult circumstances but also empowers you to grow and improve your life. Being resilient doesn't mean you won't experience difficulty or distress, but rather your inner resilience keeps you from collapsing under the stress of tragic times. Trustworthy and compassionate friends also help you navigate the necessary tasks, buoying your spirits so you can keep going during trying times.

"SHE STOOD IN THE STORM
AND WHEN THE WIND
DID NOT BLOW
HER WAY,
SHE ADJUSTED
HER SAILS."

Elizabeth Edwards

Good self-care is essential for optimal mental health. Quality self-care includes ample sleep, hydration, good nutrition, and exercise, which will not only strengthen your mind and body but will help you cope better and reduce anxiety and depression.

Practicing mindfulness and other spiritual exercises like prayer and meditation are also tools for good self-care. Others might be avoiding harmful substances, like alcohol and drugs, focusing on resources to manage your stress, seeking the help you need when you are struggling, being proactive in facing your problems, developing realistic goals, and tackling issues one step at a time.

Take the time to focus on what you can change by asking yourself the question: WHAT IS THE ONE THING I CAN ACCOMPLISH TODAY THAT HELPS ME MOVE IN THE DIRECTION I WANT TO GO? After living through a tragedy or hardship, you will have a greater sense of your inner strength, even while feeling vulnerable. Try to be rational, realistic, and avoid catastrophic thinking when you are vulnerable and exhausted.

Change is a part of life. Heraclitus, a Greek philosopher, says, *"change is the only constant in life."* As we age, some of our youthful goals and ideals may no longer be attainable. Focus on what you can change and what is important to you. It is sometimes hard to be positive when life isn't going your way, but an optimistic outlook can help you stay hopeful and positive.

Your history of suffering and defeat gives you an appreciation for calmer, uneventful days. If you are struggling, pray for the courage to believe you will weather the storm. Find the core of your inner peace to gain a positive outlook. Your strength from past challenges and failures will guide you. Bouncing back from adversity leads to optimism and gratitude. Dare to see beyond your pain to a blessed new day.

Having resilience does not eliminate stress or erase life's difficulties, and it doesn't mean that you see life through rose-colored lenses. You understand heartache, tragedy, and loss. Remember: In the face of difficulty, your resilient spirit gives you the strength you need to survive and thrive.

Ponder this thought: *"For I know the plans I have for you – this is the LORD's declaration – plans for your welfare, not for disaster, to give you a future filled with hope."*

Jeremiah 29:11

Just for Today...

Date: _____

Journaling...

Be Hopeful

Search the Horizon

SEARCH THE HORIZON

At certain times in our lives, we come to a pivotal point when we recognize the need to slow down and take the space to seek a more purposeful life. We are responding to a call for a quest for deeper meaning. When that time comes, we transcend what we know and embark on an adventure to explore the vast possibilities beyond our horizon.

Focusing on your quest, you become humbler and wiser. Taking the time to search makes you more conscious of the crucial place of generosity and kindness in your everyday life. Searching often begins with that voice inside you that says you can be what you imagine. But, you have to work, sacrifice, plan, and be patient as you seek a more genuine sense of self.

As you prayerfully engage in your pursuit of happiness, which includes not only satisfying your own needs but being aware of the needs of others, finding fulfillment in reaching out to the community and the world. It would be best if you became more outward-focused to find peace within. In giving, you will find fulfillment and satisfaction. As St. Francis tells us, *"It is in giving that we receive."*

While reaching out to others, be careful about being emotionally drained yourself, leaving you incapable of responding to another's needs. Take the time to refuel, rest and prayerfully discern ways to use your gifts and talents to help others. When you are ready to offer a helping hand, be cautious not to criticize, judge, or even attempt to wonder how those in need get into such a state of affairs. Let *"There but for the grace of God, go I"* ring loud and clear. This age-old proverbial phrase reminds you that your situation could quickly change from good fortune to a hardship, putting yourself in their situation. Strive to be empathic and respect the less fortunate with kind and gentle compassion.

Looking back over your life helps you appreciate why you made your choices, and it allows you to evaluate the price you paid for those choices. It is a humbling task, but it provides insight into how you deal with circumstances, stressors, and tensions in your life. In addition, being able to forgive yourself for your unhealthy choices helps you love and forgive others.

Your search is never over; your quest continues. Keep asking yourself the question: "WHAT DO I VALUE IN LIFE?" As you become more insightful, you will strive for a greater sense of goodness, truth, love, and happiness. In your quest, you may stumble and sometimes fall short of your aspirations. When you do stumble, you need to make that a part of your dance. It takes a long time to learn to waltz through life's challenges and still dance to the beat of a grateful heart. Tomorrow is another day to begin anew with energy and vitality to search your horizon. Sometimes your search guides you to the uncharted dreams that come true. It makes your search rewarding and worth the effort. Every day you make choices that impact how you live and the way you interact with others. Take advantage of all that lies on the horizon for you. You have options, and it is never too late to explore them. You deserve a balanced, happy life.

"THE MEANING IS LIFE IS TO FIND YOUR GIFT. THE PURPOSE IN LIFE IS TO GIVE IT AWAY."

Pablo Picasso

Continue to be open-minded and flexible. Your priorities will shift over time. What was important a few years ago may no longer be relevant. As you search your horizon, you will discover new dimensions to your quest for meaning and purpose. As you take the time to understand your past and intentionally decide on the direction of your future, continue to reach out to be a blessing to others.

Ponder this thought: *"Just beyond the horizon of the so-called impossible is infinite possibility."*

 Bryant McGill

JUST FOR TODAY...

Journaling...

Be Hopeful

"These things are true. That life derives from love, that love invites loss, that loss brings grief, that grief brings growth, and that growth means life — and so the circle is complete, and grief is a part of life. The door is open, enter life."

Paul Tschudi, Epilogue to "Grief: A Wall or a Door"

TAKE GENTLE CARE

Take gentle care as you place your hand over your heart and remember what is important for you. Pray with gratitude for your many blessings. Set realistic boundaries. You are in charge, and you get to decide how you live today. And tomorrow, when things are different, you can choose again. Beautiful things happen even amid tragedy and chaos. Sometimes your conscience is deafening with good advice. You have a choice to either listen or ignore your inner voice. Listening and responding bring inner peace. Stay the course. Stay strong.

A simple and uncluttered lifestyle is the way back to love, the way back to health, and the way back to YOU. Remember, you are special! If you want to feel healthier, come back to healthy habits without guilt for letting them go. Coming back is your connection to hope. There is healing in hope.

When I was a graduate student at George Washington University, I had a professor who stayed in touch with his students by frequent emails. Paul Francis Tschudi was on GWU's faculty in the master of Health Science and End of Life Care program. He was the faculty's connection, always available to his students. Paul ended his emails with the complimentary closing "TAKE GENTLE CARE." It meant much more to me than the typical TAKE CARE closing. I have adopted his coined phrase because of its caring implications.

Not surprisingly, Paul Tschudi was a dedicated professor who had a passion for alleviating humankind's suffering. Tragically, Paul died in a house fire a few days before this book went to print. His final Facebook posting sums up this book's purpose and is a testimony to Paul's life mission.

Paul, thank you for making a difference in my life and the lives of many. You were an enlightened soul, a humble person, a mentor, a professor, and a treasured friend. You made the world a better place with your presence. May you soar high on eagle's wings!

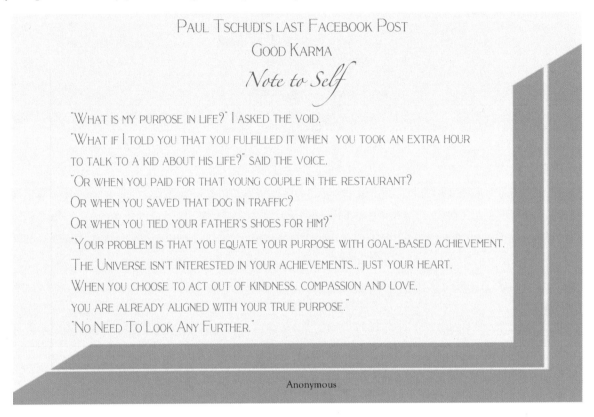

PAUL TSCHUDI'S LAST FACEBOOK POST
GOOD KARMA

Note to Self

"WHAT IS MY PURPOSE IN LIFE?" I ASKED THE VOID.
"WHAT IF I TOLD YOU THAT YOU FULFILLED IT WHEN YOU TOOK AN EXTRA HOUR
TO TALK TO A KID ABOUT HIS LIFE?" SAID THE VOICE.
"OR WHEN YOU PAID FOR THAT YOUNG COUPLE IN THE RESTAURANT?
OR WHEN YOU SAVED THAT DOG IN TRAFFIC?
OR WHEN YOU TIED YOUR FATHER'S SHOES FOR HIM?"
"YOUR PROBLEM IS THAT YOU EQUATE YOUR PURPOSE WITH GOAL-BASED ACHIEVEMENT.
THE UNIVERSE ISN'T INTERESTED IN YOUR ACHIEVEMENTS... JUST YOUR HEART.
WHEN YOU CHOOSE TO ACT OUT OF KINDNESS, COMPASSION AND LOVE,
YOU ARE ALREADY ALIGNED WITH YOUR TRUE PURPOSE."
"NO NEED TO LOOK ANY FURTHER."

Anonymous

Ponder this thought: *"Be healing with your words, be tender with your words, be gentle with your words and watch your words bring gentle, tender healing in the hearts of others."*

Heather Wolf

Just for Today...

Date: _____

Journaling...

UNDERSTANDING *"I Am Sorry"*

Saying *"I am sorry"* is an expression of remorse and an outreach for healing. Even before the uttering of the words, soul-searching begins. Processing your feelings and emotions is vital to sort out the circumstances that led to the hurt. You need to struggle with your rationalizations, excuses, justifications to get down to an honest appraisal. Yet, there comes a time when you have to admit that you were wrong, and it was your fault. By saying, *"I am sorry,"* you are taking responsibility for the hurt you caused. Sometimes the fault lies on both sides. Forgiveness needs to be extended and received to restore love and harmony. Being mutually healed is worth the awkwardness.

> "SAYING 'I'M SORRY
> IS SAYING 'I LOVE YOU'
> WITH A WOUNDED HEART
> IN ONE HAND AND YOUR
> SMOTHERED PRIDE
> IN THE OTHER."
>
> Richelle E. Goodrich

You have and will continue to make mistakes, and sometimes you don't realize that your actions cause emotional pain. When you offend someone, you need to accept responsibility and apologize. The deeper the hurt, the longer the healing process. Often, you do something and don't think of the repercussions it has for others. Saying *"I am sorry"* opens the door to communication and better understanding, and it suggests you want to make up and ask forgiveness. It doesn't automatically mean forgiveness will follow. Forgiveness takes time. The impact of our actions may have lasting effects.

Forgiveness is what you are asking for when you apologize. First, you need to forgive yourself, to make peace with yourself after doing or saying something hurtful. You need to feel remorseful and express that remorse. By forgiving yourself, you are not clearing yourself of blame but acknowledging that you did wrong. Taking responsibility and being sincerely sorry is essential to forgiveness.

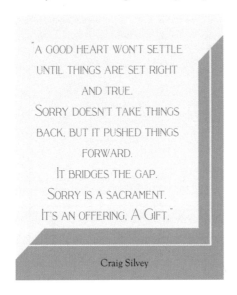

"A GOOD HEART WON'T SETTLE UNTIL THINGS ARE SET RIGHT AND TRUE. SORRY DOESN'T TAKE THINGS BACK, BUT IT PUSHED THINGS FORWARD. IT BRIDGES THE GAP. SORRY IS A SACRAMENT. IT'S AN OFFERING. A GIFT."

Craig Silvey

Expressing regret for what you have done is the beginning of being forgiven. Sometimes what you did was an oversight and unintentional, but it caused hurt and disappointment. Blaming does not lead to healing and forgiveness. A sincere apology is well received. It is a regretful acknowledgment. With a bruised heart and a deflated ego, humbly express your sorrow and ask for forgiveness. An apology is only the beginning. It helps mend broken hearts and relationships and shows respect and empathy to the wronged person. The emotional benefits allow you to move past your anger and prevent you from being stuck in the past, opening the door to forgiveness. An apology reduces the debilitating effects of remorse and shame you may feel when you hurt another.

Two sentences are essential in any relationship, "*I am sorry. Please forgive me.*" I once read the vulnerable self believes the first to apologize is the bravest; the first to forgive is the strongest; the first to forget is the happiest. WHY IS IT SO HARD TO BE THE FIRST? A wise practice is to forgive and ask forgiveness before the sun sets on the day. Harboring hurtful feelings prolongs the agony and delays the healing.

Ponder this thought: "*It takes a great deal of character strength to apologize quickly out of one's heart rather than out of pity. A person must possess himself and have a deep sense of security in fundamental principles and values to genuinely apologize.*"

 Stephen Covey

JUST FOR TODAY...

Date: _____

Journaling...

Be Hopeful

V. I. P.: Very Important Person

The affirming words: *"You are the most important person in my life, very special to my heart. I will cherish and love you forever."* are heartwarming. To be a V.I.P. (Very Important Person) in the eyes of another is something to treasure. There is only one of you, and you are beautiful in the eyes of your beholder. Amazingly, you complete someone else's story and have a remarkable story of your own. You are your own kind of beautiful. Not everyone will understand or even appreciate you as a work of art, but those who do will never forget you and value you as someone exceptional.

"IT IS NEVER TOO LATE TO BE WHAT YOU MIGHT HAVE BEEN."
Mary Anne Evans

What makes you a VIP? A gift from the moment of conception, you came into the world a blessing. You brought a uniqueness no one else can give. Even in difficult times, you left your mark through all your life experiences, good and bad, every success and failure, every moment of strength and weakness. Keep the faith! Pope Francis tells us, *"having faith does not mean having no difficulties, but having the strength to face them, knowing we are not alone."* All that you are, your talents, and the wisdom you have acquired make you unique. Your experiences help you decide who journeys with you, how you spend your time, and what you deem important. Carl Jung famously said, *"You are what you do, not what you say you'll do.*

Your vision influences what you perceive as beautiful. No one else has lived your twenty-four-hour day except you. Only you! You are one-of-a-kind, and you respond uniquely to life's happenings. No one else sees the world exactly the way you do. Sharing your perceptions of the world can unlock pearls of great wisdom for others. Your values influence your choices. To expand your horizon, reach out to understand the subtle complexities of others by listening intensely to their unique stories.

Your goals and ambitions guide how you spend your time, energy, and effort. Your passion is part of what makes you unique. Understanding your passion can help you find a path guided by your values and perceptions. Nurture the flame of your passion for keeping your purpose alive and letting your cause illuminate your path. There is no doubt; you are amazing, important, and very special.

You are here for a good reason. You may not know what it is yet, but someday it will all make sense to you. In the meantime, believe in yourself and show up to accomplish the ordinary with extraordinary touches. Love who you can, help where you can, and give what you can.

From time to time, it is good to ponder these questions: WHAT MAKES YOU UNIQUE IN THIS WORLD? WHAT ARE YOUR PASSIONS AND CAUSES? WHAT ARE THE THINGS THAT STIR THE MOST PROFOUND EMOTIONS IN YOUR SOUL?

As a person with gifts and talents, you have a responsibility to make a difference in the lives of others. You possess the greatest gift of all, the gift of affirming another. Use it to make someone else's life a little better. You live in a world that is not always kind. It is easy to forget the importance of others and your role in affirming their goodness. To validate others gives them the message that they count, they are important, and they matter. The beauty is that everyone is special. Aim to live in peace and harmony. You are not only responsible for yourself but also for the needs of others. Celebrate who you are and affirm the goodness of those around you.

Ponder this thought: *"Promise me you'll always remember: You're braver than you believe, and stronger than you seem, and smarter than you think." (Christopher Robbin to Pooh)*

A. A. Milne

JUST FOR TODAY...

Date: _____

Journaling...

Be Hopeful

Spirit

Body

Mind

Photo Credit: Studio Jolie Dance

Wellness: The Mind-Body-Spirit Connection

The mind-body-spirit connection describes the three entwined aspects of being human. The physical, mental, and spiritual combine to make you holistically who you are. The mind is not separate from the body. Mind, body, and spirit are beautifully interlinked. These three pillars inspire and inform your experiences. Seeing yourself as an integrated whole instead of a conglomerate of parts is the core component of holistic healing. The need to care for your whole self becomes apparent. When you love and care for yourself - mind, body, and spirit - your whole self works in harmony.

Mind, body, and spirit mean that your well-being comes from physical, mental, and spiritual health. To be *"healthy,"* you are called to pay attention to all three of these aspects. You are more than just your thoughts. Your mental health partly determines your physical health. It is common today that medical doctors ask you about stress and turmoil in your life when you see them for physical ailments. That's because they know to pay attention to the mind-body-spirit connection.

Psychiatrists and therapists believe people who harbor negative emotions can often make themselves physically sick. Mental health issues can manifest themselves in the body, causing disease. Your body is a barometer that indicates how things are going in all areas. It also provides the musculoskeletal structure and the vital tissues and organs that carry you through this life. True health/wellness comes when you create harmony and balance among all parts—taking time to tend to yourself as a whole person can open energy channels. These connections contribute to your spiritually sound, mentally stimulating, emotionally centered, vibrant life. Listen to your emotional and spiritual needs as you seek greater happiness, joy, health, and fulfillment. By paying attention to mind-body-spirit components, you are on your way to a more balanced self. Becca Lee eloquently states: *"If you seek peace, be still. If you seek wisdom, be silent. If you seek love, be yourself."*

Because of the pandemic stressors, it became necessary for many to resort to better wellness care and implement at-home routines to attempt some resemblance of calm and peace.

"CREATE BALANCE
NURTURE YOUR SOUL.
FEED YOUR BODY.
EXPAND YOUR MIND.
STRENGTHEN
YOURSELF."

Anonymous

It is important to exercise healthy habits daily to attain better physical and mental health outcomes so that instead of just surviving, you are *thriving.* Wellness is the harmonious connection of the mind, body, and spirit - not merely the absence of disease. Simple and healthy changes to your lifestyle will help improve your *quality of life.*

Chances are, if you look at your belief system, you will find bits and pieces of the mind-body-spirit connection already in place. It is common today to combine belief systems, home remedies, and alternative medicine. A yoga class complements your psychoanalyst session, as does your morning run, your meditation, your vegan diet, or even your weekly visits to the spa. Experience the freedom of choosing the activities that help you live holistically - mind, body, and spirit. Take it slow and give your body a chance to catch up with your mind and spirit. Be proud of how hard you are trying. May you know the blessing of God's care, peacefully guiding you through challenging times with the ease of a graceful dancer gliding in midair. Be well!

Ponder this thought: *"Every experience no matter how bad it seems holds within it a blessing of some kind. The goal is to find it."*

 Buddha

Just for Today...

Date: _____

Journaling...

XOXO: Hugs and Kisses

After more than a year of isolation, we welcome the warmth of an embrace. Hugs and kisses are outward signs of love and affection. I'm sure you've seen people sign letters, cards, emails, or text messages with XO, meaning *"hugs and kisses."* It has become a famous signatory statement.

Being denied closeness during the pandemic has been difficult. It has been especially difficult for grandparents who haven't been able to embrace their grandchildren. The vaccine is a sign of hope for reuniting and embracing safely. The lack of hugs and kisses created a void and robbed us of the emotional connections vital to our well-being. The isolation and loneliness have been some of the most stressful parts of the pandemic.

Touch is the first sense we acquire, our first language. Sometimes we need to pause and regain fluency in our first language. Touch is essential to thriving. Now, more than ever, we notice human touch in a way that we didn't before the pandemic. Blowing a kiss or waving goodbye is not the same as a physical embrace. Touch is how we first communicate as babies and is fundamental to our well-being all the years of our lives. It is a natural phenomenon to touch and be touched. The need for touch exists below the horizon of consciousness. Being deprived of touch limits our communication. Touch has a significant impact on our psychological and physical well-being. We embrace our close friends and family more than we realize. The three most common words used to describe touch are *"comfort,"* *"warmth,"* and *"love."* All express the yearnings of our hearts.

"A HUG IS A GREAT GIFT. ONE SIZE FITS ALL. AND IT IS EASY TO EXCHANGE."

Anonymous

Dacher Keltner, a University of California, Berkeley sociologist who studies the impact of touch, is concerned about social distancing's long-term implications. He says that the fabric of society is held together by even the slightest physical contact. *"Touch is as important a social condition as anything,"* Keltner says. *"It reduces stress, helping people to trust one another. It allows for cooperation. Under normal circumstances, when you feel lonely, you run the risk of stress, add to that the quarantine, and that elevates the severity."*

A warm embrace has many benefits, therapeutically affecting the mind, body, and spirit. An embrace means closeness and is the most intimate expression of love. It reinforces connections, provides a sense of safety, and improves the intensity of your understanding of belonging to another. An embrace is a form of communication that allows you to express things you cannot put into words. Embracing calms you and, for a few moments, you can forget the things and problems that stress you. It helps you overcome fear. To give and receive an embrace brings you joy and soothes your soul and the soul of another.

It's the little things in life that go a long way when it comes to showing those dearest and closest to you how much you love and care. Be generous with your hugs and kisses, and embrace more. The human connection is life-giving and healing. Hugs are both a way to celebrate and a way to provide comfort without saying a single word. There are many reasons to give a hug, but no explanation is needed. Help another to survive and thrive, give a hug, a loving embrace.

Ponder this thought: *"I will not play tug o'war. I'd rather play hug o'war, where everyone hugs instead of tugs, where everyone giggles and rolls on the rug, where everyone kisses, and everyone grins, and everyone cuddles and everyone wins."*

 Shel Silverstein

JUST FOR TODAY...

Date: _____

Journaling...

Be Hopeful

YES TO INTENTIONAL LIVING

We hunger for a greater purpose and the chance to create positive change in the world. Intentional living seems to be the buzzword in recent years, but what does it mean? DO YOU EVER GET A FEELING SOMETHING ISN'T RIGHT? DO YOU EVER FEEL YOU ARE LIVING ON AUTOPILOT? When you live in a constant state of overwhelm, you tend to overthink and stress about insignificant details. To live intentionally is to live with a sense of direction and purpose. Living with intention means choosing the path that best works for you and your lifestyle. Intentional living helps you set a course for your life rather than aimlessly wandering through it. Some intentional living examples include co-housing, ethical living, frugal living, simple living, and sustainable living. Or, it can be as simple as deciding to exercise daily and taking personal time to meditate.

"BE THE CHANGE YOU WISH TO SEE IN THE WORLD."
Mahatma Gandhi

The goal is simply to live your life with a purpose. It is about the *"Whys"* and then accepting the answers. The transformative practice of intention can help you discover a radically different, gratifying way of life. An intentional approach questions how you live authentically.

You cannot avoid all failures, but you can become more intentional about dealing with your mistakes. Failures are pauses. Don't let failures be the reason to give up on your goal to achieve intentional living. As you become more comfortable and confident with making intentional choices and being mindful of what's going on in your world, you will become aware of who you are and what you want from life. You can build a more meaningful life, which may be the most rewarding thing you've ever done.

One change won't take care of all the issues in your life, but it will give you one thing to focus on and feel more intentional about every day. Intentional living is about choosing to do something new and different and committing to it. Sometimes risks are what it takes to fulfill your dreams.

Try to be more intentional today. Choose to live, not merely to exist. Choosing to live with intention is not only about the destination, but about every path, detour, and respite of life's journey. You can start by listening to your inner voice. Starting over is sometimes necessary when you decide to live intentionally. You may discover you have been pursuing the wrong path and opt to start from scratch. It is never too late to change course. Taking a different path at any age can be rejuvenating, empowering, and life-giving. The by-product is that you can be happier and more fulfilled. Most of us are not seeking a perfect life but desire a happy life. Choose intentionally to live the happy life you desire. Deep within the recesses of your being you know what path you need to take to find your way to happiness and peace. Be still and listen!

"THE MOST WASTED OF ALL DAYS IS ONE WITHOUT LAUGHTER."

E. E. Cummings

And journaling is an excellent way to keep track of your goals. You can keep a record of your feelings and the challenges and obstacles you encounter. Begin slowly and take small steps. Pace yourself until you can see a difference. Be patient! It takes time. Stay the course. The reward for building a better life is peace and contentment. What matters is deciding what you are doing and why you are doing it, not just going where life takes you. Build Your Best Life! Be Happy!

Ponder this thought: *"Learn to be what you are, and learn to resign with a good grace all that you are not."*

 Henri Frederic Amiel

JUST FOR TODAY...

Date: _____

Journaling...

Be Hopeful

BELIEVE
THERE IS
GOOD
IN THIS
WORLD.
Be the good!

ZERO IN ON BEING THE GOOD

The past few years have been volatile in many ways. Fake news never faded. Mistrust, destructive behaviors, disregard for life, racial brutality, and escalating violence seemed to dominate the news. It is easy to lose perspective and begin to doubt, be angry, anxious, and fearful. Yet, we need to believe there is plenty of good in this world of ours. Caring people have reached out in kindness, love, and concern. As small as it may appear, smiling even while wearing a mask acknowledges a human connection. Smiling has replaced touch and sends the message, *"I notice you, and I wish you well."* We continue to be inspired by the little acts of kindness and the courageous witnessing of compassion. These are the things that touch our hearts and fill us with hope.

"GOOD PEOPLE ARE LIKE CANDLES: THEY BURN THEMSELVES UP TO GIVE OTHERS LIGHT."

Anonymous

The bag of cookies or loaf of homemade bread left at the door with a note saying, *"I am thinking of you,"* the wellness check call, the invisible smile beneath the mask detected by a twinkle in the eye, do not make the headlines. Max Erhman, in 1927, wrote the Desiderata (the Latin word for *desire.*) It contains an inspiring message of hope relevant today as the coronavirus continues to instill fear and restlessness in the hearts of many.

Believe there is good in this world, and know *you* are the reason for the good. When you show up and *be the good* by being you and living your authentic self, you influence others to do the same. As a social being, what you do and how you act impact others. Your kindness can motivate others to be kind and reach out to offer help. Your beliefs, attitudes, feelings, and actions affect those around you. *Be the good* by spreading goodness to others and inspire others to make a difference. It has a ripple effect.

Inspire others to *be the good*. The greatest gift you can give the world is to lead by example, show up as your very best, and go after your purpose with persistence. Because when you do that, you will motivate others to do the same. Do not ask what this world has to offer you, but instead what you have to offer this world. *Be the good in this world*. It is the most rewarding way to approach life, and you might change someone's life. Yes, *there is good in this world,* and you are called to *be the good* – the Desiderata – words of hope for life.

Desiderata

by Max Erhmam, 1927

Go placidly amid the noise and haste.
And remember what peace there may be in silence.
As far as possible without surrender
Be on good terms with all persons.
Speak your truth quietly and clearly;
And listen to others.
Even the dull and the ignorant;
They, too, have their story.

Avoid loud and aggressive persons.
They are vexations to the spirit.
If you compare yourself with others.
You may become vain and bitter.
For always, there will be greater and lesser persons than yourself.
Enjoy your achievements as well as your plans.

Keep interested in your own career, however humble;
It is a real possession in the changing fortunes of time.
Exercise caution in your business affairs;
For the world is full of trickery.

But let this not blind you to what virtue there is;
Many persons strive for high ideals;
And everywhere life is full of heroism.
Be yourself.
Especially, do not feign affection.
Neither be cynical about love;
For in the face of all aridity and disenchantment
It is as perennial as the grass.

Take kindly the counsel of the years.
Gracefully surrendering the things of youth.
Nurture strength of spirit to shield you in sudden misfortune.
But do not distress yourself with dark imaginings.
Many fears are born of fatigue and loneliness.
Beyond a wholesome discipline,
Be gentle with yourself.

You are a child of the universe,
No less than the trees and the stars;
You have a right to be here.
And whether or not it is clear to you,
No doubt the universe is unfolding as it should.

Therefore be at peace with God,
Whatever you conceive Him to be.
And whatever your labors and aspirations,
In the noisy confusion of life keep peace with your soul.

With all its sham, drudgery, and broken dreams,
It is still a beautiful world.
Be cheerful.
Strive to be happy.

JUST FOR TODAY...

Date: _____

Journaling...

Be Hopeful

Epilogue

T he pandemic offered me quiet time without interruptions to work on this book. Woven throughout the reflections are values and philosophies to inspire and guide you. I hope they will be thought-provoking as well as a channel for greater meaning and purpose in your life.

While working as a bereavement therapist and hospice chaplain, I had the privilege of journeying with the dying during the last few weeks and days of their lives. These encounters caused me to question my mortality and the many mysteries of life. Because death was a frequent occurrence, I often got lost in the pain and anguish of the dying and their grieving loved ones. Witnessing humanity's rawness affected my emotional equilibrium. Our history of lived experiences shapes our perspective on life situations. Our lives' journeys seem to be the blending of celebration and grief and everything in between.

As I reflected on my life's journey, I envisioned it as an excursion mapped out with a AAA TripTik. My destination stops were blessings in disguise. I traveled up and down the east coast from New England to Florida with a teaching stint in St. Croix. Before retiring, I spent nine years working with the good people in the Appalachia's foothills in Kentucky. It was a special detour inland, rich with blessings.

While in Kentucky, I had the good fortune of working with the administrative team at Our Lady of Bellefonte Catholic Hospital. Our CEO, Kevin Halter, taught me many valuable lessons. His work ethic, dedication, inclusivity, and ability to empower our team were remarkable. I witnessed the compassion and kindness of the medical staff, treating patients with the kindness they would show to their loved ones.

This past year, my TripTik appeared to be inactive due to the restrictions of the pandemic. During the isolation phase of COVID-19, I took an inward excursion to reflect on my life experiences and appreciate the meaning and purpose of my existence. With the gift of time, I questioned and discovered a lot about myself as I listened to the inner voice of my heart. This retreat experience highlighted the highs and lows of my life. I have a deeper appreciation for those who accompanied me along the way and helped me cultivate the seeds of gratitude. Life is a gift that we have one chance at living.

Forty years after my life-threatening ovarian cancer diagnosis, I still wear my anchor necklace. And I still cling to it when I am struggling, confused, or fearful. I have been so blessed. In 1981, I prayed to God for just one more year. On Christmas morning of that year, my sister Ann hugged me and wished me a Merry Christmas. I remember breaking into tears and crying, *"But I want to be here next Christmas."* My anchor necklace has served as a tangible reminder that God journeys with me during the good and challenging times. Even when I doubted God, God never abandoned me.

As you come to the end of this book, I wish you a beautiful *quality of life* all your days. I hope the reflections help you choose to live your best life, listen to your inner voice, and follow the urgings of your heart. Living through the coronavirus has been a challenging time. All kinds of suffering and losses happened because of the rippling effects of the pandemic. It will take a long time to recover. Yet, we breathe in a sigh of relief, believing the worst is behind us. Go forward with a greater appreciation of the little things in life that matter the most. And, as you live your intentional life, be patient and trust the process. What is important will be revealed in God's good time. Slow down and be still remembering the words of Robin Williams: *"Everyone you meet is fighting a battle you know nothing about. Be Kind. Always."*

St. Francis de Sales wrote a prayer of consolation and peace. you during times of struggle and when you are weary with worry. *"Be at peace and put aside all anxious thoughts and imaginations."* Be hopeful!

Prayer of St. Francis de Sales

DO NOT LOOK FORWARD
TO WHAT MIGHT HAPPEN TOMORROW.
THE SAME LOVING GOD
WHO CARES FOR YOU TODAY
WILL CARE FOR YOU TOMORROW
AND EVERYDAY.
EITHER GOD WILL SHIELD YOU FROM SUFFERING,
OR GIVE YOU
THE UNFAILING STRENGTH TO BEAR IT.

Be at peace then

AND PUT ASIDE
ALL ANXIOUS THOUGHTS AND IMAGINATIONS.

Light in the Shades of Darkness

Marguerite Patricia Gilner

With expectant hearts, we flipped the calendar to the long-awaited 2021 New Year,
Anxiously living through 2020 in isolation, with bouts of dread and exhausting fear.
Praying we emerge emotionally sound, physically intact. COVID-19 echoes systemic
Elements of shattered nerves, nightmares, and cancellations. A terrifying pandemic!
Not so novel! Our ancestors battled the 1919 influenza pandemic, a global rampage,
Infecting 500 million world-wide, tragically killing millions, mostly of advanced age.

Few escape this calamity of astronomical proportions that crushed and diminished
Our hope to greet the mundane, the ordinary, to complete projects, works unfinished.
Braving sleepless nights, restless days, tears, depressed mood and debilitating fatigue,
While dreaming of our tomorrows, the return to normalcy, graced with blissful intrigue.
Zooming lost its unique appeal, bored by movie binging, board games and puzzles,
All ways of passing time, of creating distractions, but unable to erase awful struggles.

Our faith sustains us during these challenging and uncertain times. God, we believe!
During times of sadness, loss, separations, COVID deaths, console us as we grieve.
Distraught by faded hopes, scared by the wrath of the new variants, we 'stay home',
Vaccinate, search the silence of our souls, in pursuit of courage, while being alone.
There's goodness in this world; selfless acts of kindness, reflecting gospel beatitudes.
We survived thus far, this damn pandemic, and all its anguish, with heartfelt gratitude.

Amid periods of crisis, sorrow and aloneness, wearing double masks, social distancing,
Our resilient spirits whisper promises of relief, cure for the coronavirus, while witnessing
The goodness and outreach of others, expressed and shared, unimagined months ago,
Lifting spirits, responding to unforeseen needs and compassionately leaving hearts aglow.
Healing the broken-hearted, alleviating anxious thoughts, and avoiding super spreaders
We imagine the day when, without fear, we hug and embrace, and enjoy social pleasures.

The rising sun gives birth to a new day, spreading rays of hope, filtering doubtful feelings,
Offering images of life's priceless gifts, enticing simple ways of living, envisioning healings.
Priorities shift, we SLOW down, recite mantras of gratitude, meditate and prayerfully reflect
On the course our moral compass directs, believing a vision of hopefulness will resurrect.
Precious lessons learned and cherished, affirmed by God's rich blessings never to cease,
Remembering hundreds of thousands who succumbed to this virus. Gently rest in peace!

Pause to Notice

TAKE THE TIME TO SLOW DOWN AND INTENTIONALLY PAUSE TO DISCOVER THE GIFT OF THE PRESENT MOMENT. DO NOT BE IN A RUSH AND MISS OUT ON THE BLESSINGS OF THIS MOMENT, THIS DAY.

ANCHOR YOURSELF AND STAY FOCUSED ON THE HERE AND NOW AND ENJOY THE VIEW. LET THE BEAUTY OF THE UNIVERSE SOOTHE YOUR SOUL AND NURTURE YOUR SPIRIT. MAY LOVE GUIDE AS YOU PAUSE TO COUNT YOUR BLESSINGS AND CELEBRATE THE GIFT OF NOW. LIFE IS PRECIOUS AND FLEETING.

BACKGROUND PHOTO: MARGUERITE PATRICIA GILNER OUTWARD BOUND, COLORADO ROCKIES

IN MEMORIAM

Sister Catherine Anne Cesnik, SSND

Memories of your goodness, kindness, and the talents you shared

continue to touch and inspire your loved ones

and the multitude of students you taught.

When you went home to God, our world lost a beautiful woman

who lived with great faith, valor, and conviction

Your loving spirit lives on forever in our hearts.

Until we meet again,

Rest in God's loving peace.

Acknowledgments

How do I say "*Thank You*" to all those who have touched my life and empowered me to grow in wisdom and grace and to keep going when I fell short of my expectations? First, I am most grateful to my many loved ones and dear friends who encouraged me to dream impossible dreams and chase after them with determination and perseverance. Next, I tender my gratitude to Fr. Thomas J. Donellan and Sister Patricia Gamgort, OSB, for their love, guidance, and friendship since my childhood years. They were a blessing during my youth and have been a supportive presence in my adult life.

My four nephews and their families hold a special place in my heart. Through the years, family and friends have positively influenced the ebbs and flows of the rhythmical patterns of my life. God put good people in my life for a reason, traversing many seasons. I am grateful for the friendships that have blossomed through the years. Each friend supported me during an important phase, passing the baton to another as I ventured onward on this sacred and amazing journey called *life*.

As a college student, I benefited from outstanding professors at the now Notre Dame of Maryland University. Sister Virgina Geiger, SSND, a metaphysics and philosophy professor, was one of the many exceptional faculty members. We stayed in touch over the decades. Sister gently challenged me to follow my dreams. Toward the end of her life, I was her hospice chaplain and had the privilege of spending time with Sister during her last days and was grateful to visit her a few hours before her death. With tears streaming down my face, I was able to thank her for the precious gift of her friendship. I may not recall the rudiments of logic, metaphysics, and epistemology she taught me, but I will never forget Sister Virgina's genuine interest, loving-kindness, and encouraging words.

Even at a young age. my mother often said to me, *"You go where angels fear to tread."* That has been true on many levels, a theme woven throughout my life's journey. I am a lover of wonder and awe, always believing there is more to life than the obvious. My mother knew my heart. She worried for my safety because I had no fear and was willing to take risks, even when danger was lurking.

I am grateful to Linda Fox. Linda provided the initial editing during the first phase of writing this book. Assisting in the editing process were Rod Hieneman and Thom Morris. They share the Bon Secours connection with me. Years ago, Mary Pat Gray and Dottie Weber encouraged me to pursue creative writing. I am grateful to them and treasure their friendships.

I am grateful to Gilchrist, a hospice service in Maryland, for the privilege of being part of the chaplaincy team. As chaplains, we ministered to the seriously ill and end-of-life patients and their families. The dying taught me precious lessons about living and treasuring the gift of life.

With heartfelt appreciation, I am grateful to the Sisters of Bon Secours. My family's connection with the Sisters dates back to 1918. That year, my father was a young child when a house fire severely injured him a few blocks from the Bon Secours Hospital's building site. He had the highest esteem for the two Sisters who, for months, provided home health care and nursed him back to health. He never forgot their loving kindness. It was my hope to one day become a part of the Sisters of Bon Secours' ministry. My dream became a reality in 2009 when I joined the administrative team at Our Lady of Bellefonte Hospital in Ashland, Kentucky, an affiliate of the Bon Secours Health System. During my nine years in Ashland, Kentucky, Sister Anne Lutz, CBS, served as the Chief Sponsorship Officer for Bon Secours Health System. A humble and wise leader, Sister Anne was the epitome of a calming presence in the workplace. Sister Anne has been an inspiration to all of us who had the privilege of being mentored by her.

While in Kentucky, I witnessed the dedicated leadership and the kind-hearted work of caring physicians, nurses, and staff doing God's work every day as they lived the Bon Secours mission and values. Sadly, Our Lady of Bellefonte Hospital closed in April 2020. But, I am sure the beautiful place on the hill will echo memories of compassionate care delivered with amazing grace for decades to come.

"Look to the birds of the air...

They do not sow or reap, yet your Heavenly Father feeds them."

Luke 12

"Consider the lilies of the field and how they grow.

They neither toil nor spin. Are you not of more value than they?"

Matthew 6

"Peace I leave with you;

My peace I give to you;

not as the world gives

do I give to you?

Do not let your heart be troubled,

nor let it be fearful."

John 14:27

About the Author

Marguerite Patricia Gilner grew up in Ilchester, on the outskirts of Ellicott City in Howard County, Maryland. She received her bachelor's degree from the now Notre Dame of Maryland University and is an alumna with graduate degrees from the Loyola University of Maryland, The Johns Hopkins University, and The George Washington University. She studied art design at Notre Dame of Maryland University and Barry University in Miami Shores, Florida to advance her artistic talent.

Marguerite's ministry career experiences include working as a Catholic educator, a director of palliative care initiatives, a pastoral counselor, a hospice chaplain, and a vice president of a Catholic hospital. Licensed as a clinical professional counselor, Marguerite has advocated for patient rights that improve the *quality of life* for those suffering with chronic, mental, and terminal illnesses. In 2018, she retired to the southern shore of Delaware. From her childhood years, the beach has been a place of happy memories, tranquility, and peace. Marguerite finds joy working with creative designs. *Marguerite's Treasures* is the venue she uses to share her artistic works.

HONEYSUCKLE HILL PUBLISHING

MILTON, DELAWARE

Made in the USA
Middletown, DE
08 October 2021